THE MODERN NIRVANA ORACLE

AWAKEN YOUR INTUITION AND DEEPEN YOUR AWARENESS

Kat Graham, Jennifer Sodini, Frank Elaridi, and Bryant Wood

ILLUSTRATED BY
Natalee Miller

Quotation sources and other resources can be found online at linktr.ee/modernnirvanaoracle.

ISBN 978-1-7972-1765-9

Manufactured in China.

Design by Pamela Geismar.
Typeset in Bon Vivant Serif and Brandon Text.

10 9 8 7 6 5 4 3 2 1

CHRONICLE PRISM
Chronicle Prism is an imprint of Chronicle Books LLC,
680 Second Street, San Francisco, California 94107
www.chronicleprism.com

DEDICATION

This deck is dedicated to my younger self, who was always looking for guidance, and not always in the right place. And to the youth of today who are searching for guidance and don't know where to go. —Frank Elaridi

This work is dedicated to love, the superlative human state from which all that is miraculous has the potential to be born. May this great work remind you of the transformational power of love and allow you to be liberated from the shackles of fear, so that each day of this life feels like Heaven on Earth, your very own Modern Nirvana. —Jennifer Sodini

I dedicate this deck to the version of me who still has questions. May you remember that because you can read these words right now, the answers have been inside you all along.

—Bryant Wood

I'd like to dedicate this to every healer, shaman, psychic, and friend who helped guide me through the symbols and signs that I needed to see when I felt the most lost in my life. —Kat Graham

INTRODUCTION

WHAT IS MODERN NIRVANA?

The goal of Modern Nirvana is to be a catalyst for transformation in people's lives, to inspire them to take control of their spiritual and physical well-being, by sharing both ancient practices and modern bio-hacks. Our mission is to bring inspiration and information to a new generation, paving a way for a more enlightened world.

WHAT IS AMENTI ORACLE?

"In the Emerald Tablets, the Halls of Amenti are described as being a space between worlds, where time collides, and past, present, and future potentials coexist. A crystalized codex of consciousness, which is simultaneously a hall of records and a plane of reality. This mysterious space can find its closest correspondence in the notion of the Akashic Records. The Akashic Records, like the Halls of Amenti, are viewed as a treasury of time, which stores all of the lives, memories, emotions, actions, intentions, and moments of the human and planetary experience (and evolution)." (Source: *Amenti Oracle: Feather Heart Deck and Guidebook*)

THE MODERN NIRVANA ORACLE

Merriam-Webster defines the word *synchronicity* as "the coincidental occurrence of events and especially psychic events (such as similar thoughts in widely separated persons or a mental image of an unexpected event before it happens) that seem related but are not explained by conventional mechanisms of causality."

Some spiritual teachers in the modern-day zeitgeist posit the notion that synchronicity is an echo from the universe meant to signal that we are on the right path, while others regard these ripples in time as mere coincidences that *feel* meaningful but are mostly just random iterations of reality.

Synchronicity, for the spiritual seeker, can be a helpful tool; we can think of it as a stream or current that serves as a signal boost to our consciousness, helping us reaffirm choices and moments in time. Cultivating a deeper relationship with intuition, our instincts beyond logic and reason, allows for a greater canvas to feel, see, and experience reality; it colors the imagination with meaningful coincidence and affirmative energies.

In our modern world, intuition can carry a stigma, as though it is something strange, unusual, or foreign to the human experience. Yet, this language beyond words, the language of **feeling**, exists deep within our hearts and minds, whether we are conscious of it or not. This sight beyond vision can appear as an apparition in a dream; a download of information (without having previous knowledge); an inner gut feeling about a person, place, or thing; or an instant recognition of a kindred connection that we know will forever change the trajectory of our lives.

Phenomena such as synchronicity, intuition, precognition, and divination refer to ways of being and knowing that transgress the empirical and rational logics of our modern and linear materialist worldviews. Yet many of us come to believe, as a result of our life experiences, that the prevalent maps and models of the world do not account for the whole of reality. And indeed, throughout the ages, human beings have searched for answers from beyond and have hoped to peer behind the curtain of consensus reality through various mediums and/or messengers.

Historically, the agency and mediation of oracles were one of the most widespread and universal methods to peek beyond the veil, as it were. The word *oracle* comes from the Latin verb *ōrāre*, "to speak," and refers to the person or entity who is able to recover information from realms beyond sensory perception, sharing it with their fellow humans. Oracles have been the voice of gods and goddesses, spirits and demons, deceased ancestors, extraterrestrial entities, and plants and animals. The utility of the oracle has found its way through various wisdom traditions, cultures, and systems of divination across the globe and throughout history.

In ancient Greece, the Pythia (or Pythoness) was the name given to the oracle, a female high priestess who served as a medium for messages from beyond. It was said that within the Temple of Apollo in Delphi, there was a chasm where the oracle performed her ritual. She sat on a tripod so she could inhale the vapors that came through the crack in the Earth. This process put her into a trancelike state, where her voice became more than human and she would tell prophecies that needed to be analyzed and deciphered.

John Dee (1527–1608/9) was a master alchemist, astrologer, magician, mathematician, and scientist who served as "conjurer" and adviser to Queen Elizabeth I. In his secret correspondences with Elizabeth I, Dee signed his letters as 007, a code indicating that the message was for her eyes only. He believed the 0s represented eyes and the 7 gave luck. The original—and metaphysical—James Bond, Dee was a scholar of Hermeticism and the occult, and at one point was revered as one of the most learned men in England. He also believed that he, along with his colleague Edward Kelley, could communicate with angels using a black obsidian scrying mirror, which allowed him to channel their ancient and mystical language, Enochian.

In the Shipibo tradition of the Amazon rainforest, sacred plants act as a link between human and other-than-human worlds. The plants allow the Onanya ("the one who knows," in the Shipibo language) to commune with the wisdom of the rainforest and receive guidance and medical knowledge from the plants themselves in order to heal their patients. When under the influence of these medicines, the healers perceive themselves as empty vessels who channel the spirits of the trees and plants they have previously dieted, directing them through their Ikaros, the medicine songs and melodies that are unique to each plant. Guided by the plants, the Onanya heals and offers counsel.

Throughout the Himalayas, oracles play an important part in mystical revelations of prophecy and religious doctrine. The Nechung Oracle is a human medium who goes into trance and becomes possessed by Pehar, a former evil spirit who was transformed into a bodhisattva and protector of Buddhism. Pehar speaks through the medium in order to confer with leaders on matters of state, governmental decision-making, intelligence, and security.

> Young Monk: "Do not try and bend the spoon—that's impossible. Instead, only try to realize the truth."
> Neo: "What truth?"
> Young Monk: "There is no spoon."
>
> —*The Matrix* (1999)

In Lana and Lilly Wachowski's film *The Matrix*, there is a famous scene where the protagonist, Neo, goes to visit a character called "The Oracle." While Neo is in her apartment, the ancient Greek aphorism *Temet Nosce* ("Know Thyself") can be read hanging above the kitchen door. The Oracle does not offer Neo tangible answers, but instead, she speaks in riddles, which offer more questions. Her insight is expressed like puzzle pieces for Neo to piece together through his own experience as he embarks on the Hero's Journey to find out who he really is and what he is truly capable of. Some have viewed *The Matrix* as a modern-day commentary on Plato's Allegory of the Cave, which is an imaginative exploration of the relationship between perception and reality. The Oracle knows that while certain things have to be seen to be believed, they also must be believed in order to be seen; our perception shapes our reality and vice versa.

The common thread in these stories throughout history is that the seeker is searching for information from an outside source—another person, a medium beyond their own power, a conduit beyond their own consciousness. While it is important not to discount the potency of a divine messenger, it is equally important to realize, and actualize, the power that exists within **you** as your own messenger, divine instrument of creation, and generator of intuition and insight.

> **"A baby has brains, but it doesn't know much. Experience is the only thing that brings knowledge, and the longer you are on earth the more experience you are sure to get."**
> —L. Frank Baum, *The Wonderful Wizard of Oz*

And, with all of this in mind, dear reader, Modern Nirvana and Amenti Oracle have joined forces to create *The Modern Nirvana Oracle* as a tool of self-inquiry and empowerment through life's transitions. The collaborative vision of Kat Graham, Jennifer Sodini, Frank Elaridi, and Bryant Wood that exists within the deck has been designed to offer clarity around the gradients of love, loss, levity, and each chapter of the human experience. Using grace, openheartedness, and a holistic worldview, this deck intends to open the mind and spirit to new realms of perspective. With an aesthetic inspired by esoterica and avant-garde '80s fashion (what we have playfully dubbed *Ancient Vogue*), Natalee Miller's art drives home the sensory experience for the heart and imagination to be open to new possibilities.

Attaining Nirvana, from an esoteric point of view, is the liberation of the spirit from the cycles of suffering and karma, becoming free of attachment, yet connected to the ineffable interconnectedness of all things. Our greatest hope and intention is for this deck to help liberate your spirit so you can attain a sense of grounded enlightenment by tapping into your inherent wisdom, allowing your questions to be your guide, and answering the call to find your highest self. We hope this collaborative vision is a vehicle of transformation that teaches you how to identify (and work with) signals of synchronicity, refine your intuition, polish your inner mirror, and redefine your role as an active creator and adept navigator of our increasingly complex but incredibly beautiful world.

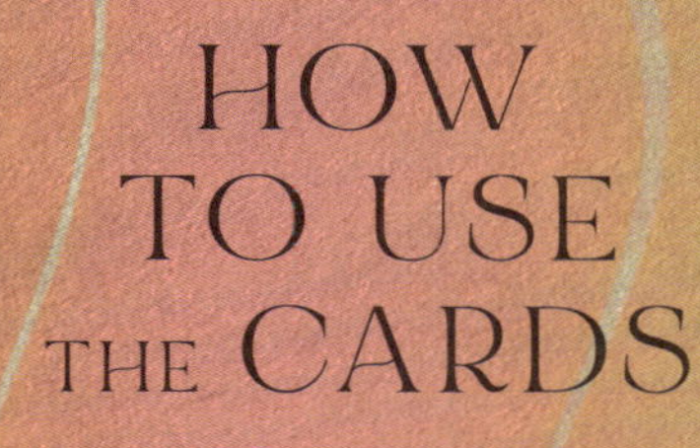

HOW TO USE THE CARDS

Some of life's greatest answers can be found in the questions themselves.

Who am I?
What is my purpose?
Why am I here?

Existential inquiry is inherent to the human experience, and while we may not always get binary answers to the **big** questions, having an array of tools in our metaphysical toolkits can help unpack the gray areas as we delve deeper into the layers of guidance we are working through.

> **"'Who in the world am I?' Ah, *that's* the great puzzle."**
>
> —Lewis Carroll,
> *Alice's Adventures in Wonderland*

These oracle cards have been designed to offer guidance, easily digestible teachings, and practical bits of esoteric wisdom inspired by Eastern philosophy, and sprinkled throughout the deck you will also find ten meditative practices to further ground the symbolic language and art within this journey.

Each of these ten cards is coupled with a sigil (a symbol imbued with power, used often in magickal practice) to assist in activating the intention of the words by embossing the subconscious mind with an illustrated intention.

Every card has a prescient quote to tickle the imagination and inspire. Within each passage, you will also find a mantra, a word that in Hinduism means a sacred phrase or message. These mantras are designed to bring another level of perception to your reality as you repeat the words from your heart center. Spend time with each mantra; say it out loud or in your head until you feel a visceral reaction in your body. Each time you say the mantra, the power of it is strengthened.

The clearer you are when asking the cards questions, the more clarity you may find in relation to what you receive back from your consciousness.

There may be days where your heart is overflowing with questions about love, work, health, relationships, or what to **do**, but sometimes, less can be more when it comes to finding a deeper connection, or a guiding light on the path, that brings us closer to wholeness. If you find that you're at an inner impasse with what you're seeking clarity on, sometimes a simple intention instead of a question can go a long way. For example, telling the cards, "I am open to receive," can unlock unexpected answers.

PREPARING YOUR MODERN NIRVANA DECK

The saying **"energy goes where attention flows"** can be a useful mantra when it comes to working with the cards, what type of energy or attention you imbue into your practice, and the relationship you build with this deck.

1. CLEAR YOUR ENERGY

Find a quiet space where you can focus your complete attention on the present moment. Sit cross-legged or on your knees with the deck in front of you. Imagine a bright gold light, taking the shape of a figure eight between you and the cards, connecting you energetically.

Close your eyes and shift your awareness from the outside world to your own mental, physical, and emotional landscape. Now imagine a cord emerging from the gold light, which connects as a grounding tether to your solar plexus (the space between your rib cage and your navel). It moves deep into the Earth, wrapping around its core, so that you feel firmly supported and connected with your environment.

With three expansive breaths, visualize in your mind's eye your body rising above the edge of the universe in a pillar of white light that you bring into your body and back down through every cell and into the Earth. You are now connected and communicative with your higher self.

2. CLEAR THE CARDS

If possible, light sustainably sourced sage or palo santo, or place a charged crystal directly upon the cards. Imagine all karmic forces and past intentions releasing from the deck while calling in grace, ease, and the highest good for yourself and all sentient beings.

Do this by meditating upon the color of your own energy. (If you're unsure what that may be, close your eyes and ask to be shown what that color is.) While breathing into your heart, push that color through your hands onto the cards.

You can do this while holding the cards in your left hand or by simply laying both hands gently on the deck. Do this until you feel your own energy and the card's energy become one and the same. These cards are now an extension of you, and the answers these cards provide come from answers that have always been within you.

3. CUT THE DECK/PULL CARDS

The pharaonic stance is left foot forward; it symbolizes the ability to lead with the heart.

In this tradition, you would pick up the cards with your left hand and shuffle them by gently placing them out of order (do not "Vegas shuffle" your cards—they can capture stray energies or become easily damaged), then place them back in front of you.

Cut the deck three times, again with your left hand.

Put the deck back together, lay out the cards for the reading you wish to do, and turn them, also with your left hand.

Now, you're ready to begin!

SAMPLE SPREADS

Whether you're looking for a quick hit of inspiration by pulling one or two cards to meditate on or seeking deeper guidance, we have created three sample spreads to accompany the work and kindle your intuition.

As you get to know the cards, we encourage you to experiment and formulate your own spreads based on the intentions of your questions and the guidance you're looking to receive on your path of self-inquiry. Two of these spreads are inspired by Buddhism, while the third is inspired by the elements in nature. You can create a unique card spread using almost anything as a source of inspiration! Let your imagination, heart, and questions be your guide.

It may take some getting used to, but in time, you will find your flow and make the cards, and the practice, your very own.

THE THREE JEWELS

In Buddhism, the Three Acts of Refuge (or the Three Jewels) are the Buddha, the Dharma, and the Sangha.

The Buddha represents not only the historical Buddha, but teachers who also inspire a "remembering" of our own inner Buddha Nature and potential for enlightenment. One could consider the concept of Buddha Nature as our inherent ability to blossom into greatness of spirit because of the divine seed of consciousness we each possess in the brilliance of our minds.

The Dharma represents the teachings, which reflect upon the basic truth of reality and the various stages, duties, and principles we exist in as we move through life as spiritual beings having human experiences.

The Sangha represents the community aspect of the spiritual path being an integral part of the applied learning, integration, and embodiment of the teacher and the teachings.

With these concepts in mind as metaphors of self-inquiry, posit these questions as you shuffle, and then pull three cards.

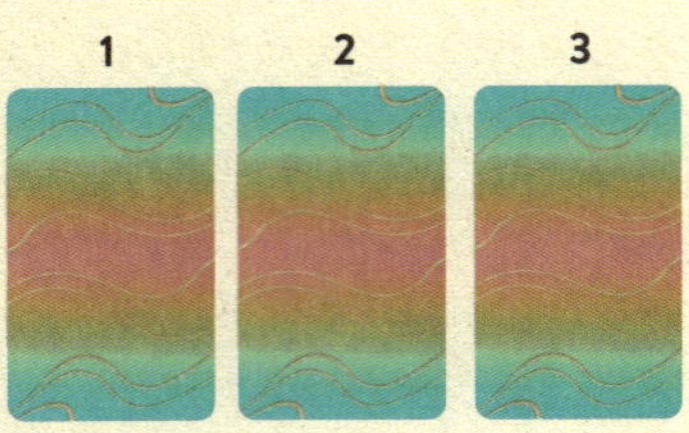

1. **What is preventing me from connecting to my own Buddha Nature?**
2. **What is the most important action for me to take in my daily life so that I can be of service to others?**
3. **How can I find a deeper connection to my community at this moment in time?**

NOBLE TRUTH

After the Buddha found enlightenment, one of his first profound realizations centered around the idea that suffering and life are inextricably linked.

Understanding the keys that exist within the truths of suffering can open doors to liberation from that which makes us suffer.

This spread has been designed to question the root of adversity in our lives so that we may tend to our attachments and cultivate a deeper sense of peace and liberation from our fears.

Shuffle the cards to your liking while reflecting on these questions, then pull four cards to receive your guidance.

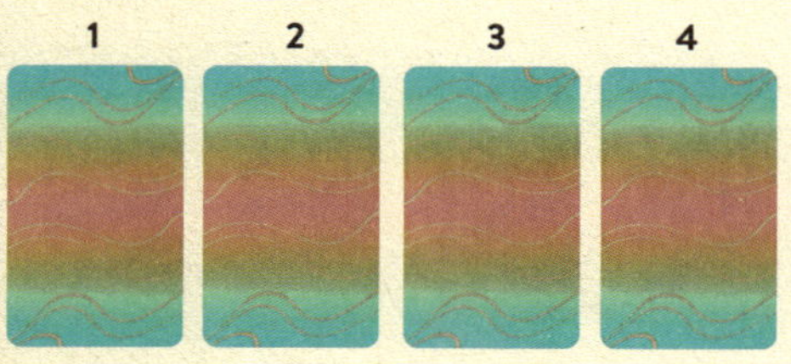

1. **How am I suffering in this current moment?**
2. **How can I create ease and peacefulness around this distress?**
3. **What is the lesson this experience is here to teach me?**
4. **How can I best embody the frequency of liberated presence?**

THE FIFTH ELEMENT

In many esoteric practices and magical traditions, looking to the elements as a source of symbolism and strength grants an understanding of self in relationship to nature.

Earth symbolically represents a grounded connection between ourselves and our environment.

Air represents our mental faculties and links us to a greater life-force energy.

Fire can symbolize strength, desire, and the energy we empower ourselves with to complete our greatest goals.

Water represents our subconscious beliefs, our intuition, and our dream spaces.

This spread encourages a connection between self and the elements we each can embody, with a final prompt unifying each of their properties, synthesizing through loving awareness, and looking at love as the Fifth Element.

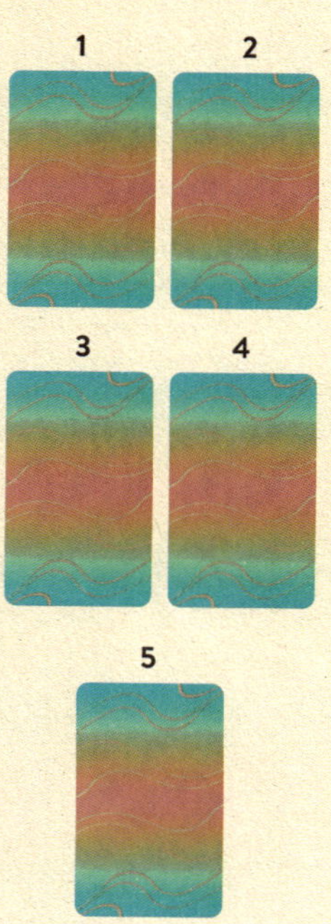
1
2
3
4
5

1. What do I need in order to stay grounded and connected to the Earth?
2. How can I remember to live in awareness of my breath, allowing the ever-present energies of Air to envelop my emotions when I feel disconnected from love?
3. What should I ignite more of in my life to feed the Fire of my deepest desires?
4. How can I remain fluid in times of conflict so I can continue to navigate my life with the power of Water (as a metaphor) in mind?
5. How can I best embody love as an action—by being, doing, seeing, feeling, and revealing my highest purpose for the benefit of all beings?

CARD DEFINITIONS

ABUNDANCE

"Simplicity, patience, compassion. These three are your greatest treasures."

—Lao Tzu, *Tao Te Ching*

Allow the feeling of abundance to wash over you.

Focus on all of the incredible blessings of your life. Feel your heart beat and your breath move. Do you have all of your senses? Do you have food on the table, a bed at night? Find the abundance in the little things!

Materialism can be a distraction that pulls us away from our true essence. Ask yourself at this moment what you truly have in abundance.

Life? Love? Family? Friendships?

As much as you can, live in a state of appreciation of your abundance. It is often from that space where you believe that you are blessed and live in contentment that unexpected blessings arrive. —KG

MANTRA: ***My life is abundant, and I am deeply appreciative of all my blessings.***

ASSERTIVENESS

"One is never afraid of the unknown; one is afraid of the known coming to an end."
—Jiddu Krishnamurti, *Freedom from the Known*

There will be many times in life where we will be met with lessons, challenges, and moments that may test our ability to keep courage through conflict and maintain balance in the metaphorical wobble of the Earth.

Uncertainty can be a source of insecurity. In situations we are unable to control, we may find ourselves defaulting to what feels comfortable, such as staying quiet or retreating into thought-loops of all the worst-case scenarios. Perhaps you diminish your light out of fear that you may burn too bright or blind others with your truth.

Are you currently in a cycle of continuing to play small?

Are you repressing your true feelings because you fear rejection?

Are you afraid of saying what you really need to get what you truly want?

Are you afraid, period?

If you pull this card, it is here to remind you that assertiveness is not to be feared, but instead to be integrated, lived, and appreciated like an invisible safety net to protect you from the unexpected or when you think you may fall.

Assertiveness is the assurance that you are worthy, you matter, you count, you absolutely deserve to be heard, and you can fully trust your forward momentum. Being assertive should not be mistaken for being aggressive or arrogant. It is the metaphysical tool that allows you to walk along the tightrope of life with a balanced heart, mind, spirit, ego, intuition, logic, and instinct.

In Joseph Campbell's famed *The Hero's Journey*, the Threshold Guardian is an archetype that prevents the hero from experiencing a new beginning. Fear is a threshold guardian that nobody is impervious to, yet we can all conquer it through the practice of asserting who we are, what we are, and why we deserve to pass through any gate we may encounter.

Learning how to embody assertiveness will allow you to know that the unknown isn't to be feared, but instead can remind you of your greatness and the greatness you can bring to a world of your own creation.

This world is yours to design and participate in, and your myth is your magic. —JS

MANTRA: ***It is safe for me to be assertive! I trust that my needs will be met and my voice will be heard.***

AUTHENTIC EXPRESSION

"Your mind transcends limitations, your consciousness expands in every direction, and you find yourself in a new, great, and wonderful world."

—Patanjali, *The Yoga Sutras of Patanjali*

Your whole body is a sacred instrument with a deep desire to express authenticity and transcend all limitations. In the divine cosmic orchestra of creation, in order to awaken the consciousness that is dormant, we must also learn how to awaken to our most authentic expression of self so we can be in harmony with our highest visions.

Today you have pulled this card because you are spending too much time in your head and may have lost touch with your heart center. This card signals the need to clear the cobwebs in your consciousness, become more grounded, and meet this moment as your truest self, unified in heart and mind. This card comes with a reminder of a powerful practice to bring your **awareness into the**

body. By allowing your natural self to act freely, your limitless potential will organically express into your reality, and blessings of abundance will follow.

Step 1: Breathe in deeply through your nose, all the way into your feet, and up to the crown of your head.

Step 2: Exhale through your nose from the crown of your head all the way into the center of the Earth.

Step 3: Inhale from the center of the Earth, through your body, all the way up past the farthest star.

Step 4: As you exhale, come into your body fully and express yourself exactly the way you would want to, as if this were your last exhale on Earth. Feel, express, love.

Step 5: Continue to breathe into your whole body exactly the way you want to breathe, and exhale with as much pleasure, grace, and bliss as you can feel.

Step 6: Let each breath become more powerful, and come into your own with each inhale.

This is the breath of the highest essence of essential awareness and can be used as a key to unlock the door to your most authentic expression of self.

When you feel that essence of authentic mind, body, and spirit slipping away, repeat this as needed. This is a practice you can return to time and time again so that you can continue to remember who you truly are. —BW

MANTRA: *I am grounded. I am aware. I am present. I embody essential awareness, and I am fully connected to my most authentic expression of self.*

AWARENESS

"The ultimate value of life depends upon awareness and the power of contemplation..."

—Aristotle

Awareness cannot exist as long as you believe that you completely know who you are and understand everything, but if you are open to infinite potential, without limitation, it may then become present in your consciousness.

In Deepak Chopra's meditations, he often has the meditator ask, **"Am I aware?"** That question is powerful, yet it cannot be explained as beautifully as it can be experienced directly. Take a moment to contemplate the question: **"Am I aware?"**

There is a difference between alertness and awareness. **Alertness** relates to the perception of physical reality through the senses. **Awareness**, however, makes even daily life a completely different experience. If you try to forcefully raise awareness, it won't happen, but if you focus on raising your vibration intentionally, then awareness will come. —FE

MANTRA: *I am conscious. I embody awareness.*

BOAT

"Mastering others is strength. Mastering yourself is true power." —Lao Tzu, *Tao Te Ching*

Your "boat" will sink only by allowing in water from the outside.

Regardless of any storm on the horizon, unless you allow the waves to fill your boat or create holes within your boat itself, you **will** rise.

Don't misinterpret the weather or waters as anything other than the environment you may be currently sailing through.

In time, the tide will settle, the clouds will part, and the sun will rise and shine again. Nothing is permanent, and nothing is introduced into your life by accident.

Every drop of water or push in a new direction is the universe guiding you to a deeper understanding. The storm is a teacher that is here to remind you to keep peace in your boat and be an observant student. —KG

MANTRA: ***I trust the direction of the universe and maintain peaceful awareness through all conditions.***

BREATH

"Feelings come and go like clouds in a windy sky. Conscious breathing is my anchor."

—Thich Nhat Hanh, *Stepping into Freedom: Rules of Monastic Practice for Novices*

Each moment of the day, you have a metaphorical sword at your hip called conscious breathing. It's a powerful tool that can help slay limiting beliefs, critical thoughts, and many of your toughest inner demons.

Any thought created by the mind can be exhaled, and released, through the breath.

Any intention you wish to bring into your reality can be inhaled and integrated through this powerful practice.

To transition from one state to another, all we have to do is shift our pattern of inhaling and exhaling with intent. This is true alchemy: learning how to use our internal systems to direct our emotions toward what feels good and most aligned with our greatest visions.

The quality of your decisions is enhanced when you act from a place of fully integrated wholeness. With breath, we have the potential to feel our best even in the darkest of times.

If you expand in the situation that scares you and choose to feel your most infinite, you reclaim your power within that experience. We are not only breathing air; we are also breathing in pure creative potential, or life-force energy.

Your internal state is your external stage, and your breath gives you the chance to design and direct the background from where you operate.

Does each moment fill you with love, strength, and wisdom? Are you consciously choosing the character you're playing in the reality of your own design?

If you pull this card, it is telling you to pay attention to your most intimate form of communication with life: breath.

Inhale the adventure and exhale your freedom.

Create your world from within by using this tool to become a master of your destiny, as you continue to move closer to realizing your dreams. The element of wind is with you and is blessing your journey ahead, allowing air's invisible current to carry you into experiences beyond your wildest imagination. It will help you soar to new heights.

How are you breathing life today? —BW

MANTRA: *I'm an alchemist of my reality and the hero of my journey. Every inhale brings golden awareness to my life, and every exhale releases that which no longer serves my highest purpose. I trust how life is breathing my spirit and where the flow is taking me.*

COMPASSION

"Compassion is an action word with no boundaries." —Prince, *Vegetarian Times* (1997)

The etymology of the word *compassion* stems back to the Latin word *compati*, which translates to "suffer with." *Merriam-Webster* gives the modern definition of the word as "sympathetic consciousness of others' distress together with a desire to alleviate it."

The Gautama Buddha identified suffering as one of the Four Noble Truths of his teachings. In viewing compassion as a spiritual practice, it is our conscious empathy for others' suffering, because of our awareness of our own degrees of suffering, that brings us closer to our shared humanity. None of us are impervious to experiencing pain as we grow through life; it is an inevitable and inherent part of the human condition and experience. With the healing that can come with acceptance and understanding, a fluency of greater feeling can be found.

The Metta Prayer of Loving-Kindness (*metta* is a Pali word meaning "good will") is a helpful meditative practice that can inspire a greater sense of compassion for all sentient beings traveling through time and space.

Let us weave this prayer's intention into a meditative breathing pattern and make it our own.

Step 1: Inhale and repeat, "May all beings everywhere be happy."

Exhale and repeat, "May all beings know true happiness."

Step 2: Inhale and repeat, "May all beings everywhere be healthy."

Exhale and repeat, "May all beings know true health."

Step 3: Inhale and repeat, "May all beings everywhere be at peace."

Exhale and repeat, "May all beings know true peace."

Step 4: Inhale and repeat, "May all beings everywhere be free."

Exhale and repeat, "May all beings know true freedom."

Step 5: Take a deep breath in, and on the exhale repeat, "All are happy, all are healthy, all are at peace, and all are free."

Move forward with compassion and continue to radiate loving-kindness to all you meet and are met with. You may begin to notice subtle changes in your heart, mind, and spirit through the love you extend and subsequently magnetize. Take note of how this energy finds its way back into your spiritual center, and how your empathy and compassion continue to expand with warm awareness. —JS

MANTRA: *I am happy, I am healthy, I am at peace, and I am free. You are happy, you are healthy, you are at peace, and you are free. We are now liberated from our suffering; once blind, now we can truly see.*

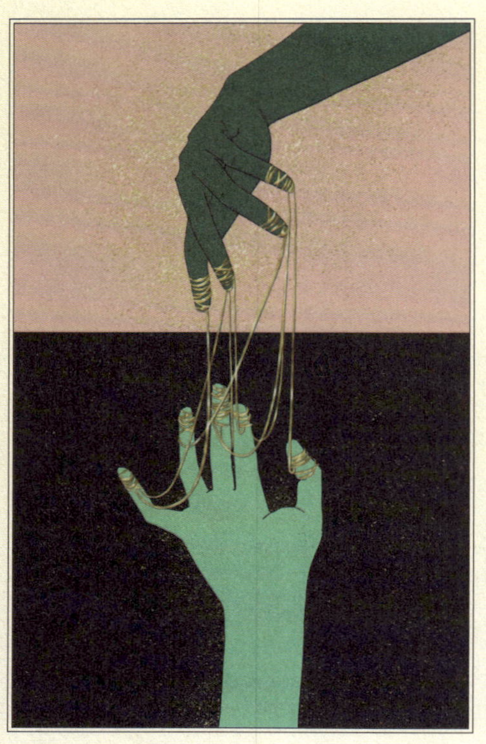

CONNECTION

"An invisible thread connects those who are destined to meet, regardless of time, place, or circumstance. The thread may stretch or tangle but it will never break."

—Chinese proverb

Have you ever connected with someone for the first time, and instead of it feeling like an initial meeting, it felt like a reunion, a remembering, or a rekindling of something that was lost? An instant recognition of a kindred spirit, a familiar resonance, or a reminder of unfinished business, where you can't quite place the **why** or **how**, but there's an understanding of a great importance that transcends all logic. You aren't sure **what** is going to happen, or **when**, but there's an inner knowing that this "chance" meeting is not by chance at all!

You may feel a sparkle of energy move through your entire body, a wave of wonder or pure emotion, or the hairs on your skin will stick straight up with goosebumps, because it feels so surreal in this moment of inexplicable knowing.

If you pulled this card, it is to remind you to be aware of a new connection on the horizon that will assist in your journey into becoming. It can also be viewed as a signifier to affirm a connection that already exists that evokes a similar fated feeling, which you may have previously questioned or shook off as random.

This connection will not only be meaningful in the future, but may also offer context and meaning for the past and present. This auspicious conduit can be perceived as a metaphorical part of fate's invisible thread of connectivity, which will continue to weave together loose ties and create a tapestry of the moments in time that are a greater part of the life of your story.

Take note of your feelings and make sure not to discount potential with doubt.

Trust your intuition and what you instinctively feel, know, and see. Sometimes the first response is actually the correct one. Don't overthink what came first organically.

The connection at hand will only grow stronger as time goes on, and the fabric of this connection will prove to be fortuitous on your journey into a bold new horizon.

Be confident, and trust the weaving. —JS

MANTRA: *I trust the tapestry of my life's design. I am in full faith that every moment and experience is threaded by the divine.*

DÉJÀ VU

"Once upon a time, I dreamt I was a butterfly . . . conscious only of my happiness as a butterfly, unaware that I was myself. Soon I awaked, and there I was, veritably myself again. Now I do not know whether I was then a man dreaming I was a butterfly, or whether I am now a butterfly, dreaming I am a man."

—Zhuangzi

Have you ever found yourself caught in a moment that feels both incredibly foreign and familiar? Like a scene from a dream trickling into reality, or a drop of rain from the clouds of the collective consciousness meeting your skin and awakening sensation.

Where did this moment come from? Has this happened before?

Déjà vu translates to "already seen," and if this card is being called into your reality, it may be time to pause and reflect on moments that have recently happened where you may have felt as though you've sliced into the breadth of time.

When déjà vu presents itself in your experience, take note of when it is happening, while also taking inventory of what is at the forefront of your consciousness. Who has this happened with, and what feels so significant about the moment? Is there a common theme in the familiarity?

Are you considering a big change, like a new job or a move out of state?

What is your current baseline of emotion and feeling?

Have you connected with a new potential partner, either romantically or in business?

Is your life generally in harmony or discord?

What are you currently desiring that is echoing out into the universe?

How are your thoughts reflecting in your reality, and how are they affecting your day-to-day experience?

Déjà vu is like the sense of calm before the storm—the changes in air, temperature, and pressure that allow us to prepare for the thunder and lightning; the insight before the shift; the umbrella before the rain.

Whatever the weather may be, pause and meditate on whether this is the path you feel you are truly being called to move toward, and prepare accordingly. Eventually, a rainbow will appear and offer its own alchemical gold through the wisdom and insight gathered in this passage of time. —JS

MANTRA: *I trust the invisible whispers, which offer guidance on my path. I choose to merge with the time line that is meant to serve my highest good.*

DIRECTION

"Your heart knows the way. Run in that direction." —Rumi

Navigating the waters of life can often be a daunting task.

Even when we think we can do no wrong, experiences pop up and make us question our understanding.

As long as you are heading in the direction of your true purpose—a purpose that is higher than yourself and benefits mankind—then you are walking in the right direction, and support is on its way.

Trust that you are moving in accordance with the source of all things.

Trust that any missteps are only detours to make the right path impossible to avoid.

Regardless of how uncomfortable the road is, how high the waters are, or how hot the flames along the path are, walk forward with conviction, passion, and trust. —KG

MANTRA: ***I am heading in the right direction and fully trust the path ahead.***

DISCERNMENT

"You don't actually 'become' a buddha, you simply cease, slowly, to be deluded. And being a buddha is not being some omnipotent spiritual superman, but becoming at last a true human being."

—Sogyal Rinpoche, *The Tibetan Book of Living and Dying*

When we are called to reflect on the idea of discernment, we are asked to seek presence and exercise good judgment in mind, body, and spirit. But how do we know what is **good** or **bad** when it comes to our choices and actions? What is **good** or **bad** when it comes to our judgments? What is truly **good** or **bad** not just subjectively, but objectively speaking? How do we harmonize the various aspects of our human vessel so that we can think, feel, and be our very best?

Working on our ability to listen, observe, and absorb allows us to integrate information from a holistic point of view. By transcending reactivity and emotion, we can find a relationship with equanimity, or the state of overall mental calmness. If we view **good** as a positive outcome of any experience we are flowing through, equanimity can present itself as the evolved result.

The classic Mahayana Buddhist teaching on Dharma, the Three Vessels, uses three pots as a visual analogy for the importance of listening and retaining how we process and receive information through our metaphorical vessels.

The upside-down pot asks us to remember to listen to life's teachings, without distraction or assumption, so we can fully absorb the lesson at hand.

The pot with a hole reminds us of the importance of integrating what we listen to, instead of letting information leak out without being retained, embodied, and practiced.

The poison pot tells us to keep an open mind and heart, free from projection and what in Buddhism is called the Five Poisons, which are attachment, aversion, ignorance, jealousy, and pride.

When discernment shows up as a teacher, remembering the Three Vessels and connecting to their lessons can allow stability and graceful composure to make its way into your heart even through the most challenging of situations. Transmuting the poisons into a precious perspective allows nonattachment, openheartedness, wisdom, compassion, and humility to emanate from our presence and flow forward to all of the lives we touch with this loving awareness. —JS

MANTRA: *I am committed to unifying with the most authentic expression of loving awareness. I am aware that integration is integral to maintaining this embodiment of truth. I listen, I hear, and I fully understand.*

ECSTASY

"When you are inspired by some great purpose, some extraordinary project, all your thoughts break their bonds." —Patanjali

What does it *really* mean to enjoy all aspects of life?

What would it feel like to be in an ecstatic space of joy each day you're alive on this Earth?

If you have to do something, it is worth learning how to enjoy the very process of doing (and being), by meeting that experience with a blissful spirit. At times, the universe will accept counterfeit emotion for currency and will respond in kind. If you make the best of things you dislike but have been called to follow through with, your relationship with them will change. Take note of these changes and where you can find value in the lessons of playing pretend or living in the space of playfulness, flow, and being in joy.

Where are you discovering genuine delight in the authentic reality of your emotions?

Rising above what you fear is an alchemical process of transmutation. It is important to remember that it is always darkest before dawn, there is usually more chaos before there is order, and sometimes things need to dissolve in order to design something new. If you can lean into discomfort with an attitude of openness to the exciting current of the unknown, you may be pleasantly surprised by the ecstatic release that exists on the other side of uncertainty.

The Ecstasy card is a sign to reclaim old joy or find it anew, and to not be discouraged in this pursuit of what brings you the most pleasure and connects you to your true bliss.

If you have grief or sadness blocking your path to ecstasy, remember that grief may just be love in disguise and is a guide to moving through old obstacles. It is important to remember that love is stronger than any illusion or mirage of the mind! Each obstacle can be perceived as a temporary moment instead of a story that feels burdensome. If you learn to make friends with what is, your relationship to the entire journey of what can be will change.

Watch your life transform through the ecstasy you allow, and witness how the euphoria of an open heart will unlock new horizons. —BW

MANTRA: ***I approach life with an open heart, and remain open to my highest excitement and ecstatic experiences.***

EMOTIONS

"I've learned that people will forget what you said, people will forget what you did, but people will never forget how you made them feel." —Unknown

When emotions, such as fear and anxiety, are intensely felt, they can become trapped in the body. While we are not always aware of them, they manifest in our relationships, our work, and other areas of life.

You don't realize how heavy the emotions you carry actually are until you put them down. And that is the beautiful news—you **can** put them down.

Energy healing has been used for thousands of years, but many people today are disconnected from it and are not aware that they can access these holistic practices. You can harness the power of energy healing and unlock the body's natural ability to correct misalignments and imbalances that may lead to physical and emotional symptoms.

Dr. Bradley Nelson teaches a process called "The Emotion Code," which gives people the ability to learn how to clear negative trapped emotions in the body and rid themselves of unseen baggage.

Today, let us try an “Emotion Code” exercise to introduce ourselves to the practice of self-healing using energy work. Get comfortable and meditate on what you feel right now. Allow yourself to feel it fully and without judgment. The reason some emotions get trapped in the body to begin with is because they went unprocessed, so this is your opportunity to process what it is you are feeling.

Really take your time, and once a clear emotion is identified and felt, notice where in the body you feel the emotion, then put your hand in that spot. Give this area of the body some love like you would a child’s scraped knee. Acknowledge the emotion. Thank it for being there to help you on your path.

Now swipe your hand over the spot three times and energetically release the emotion, feeling it disappear. Next, rub your hands together until they feel warm and cup your face in the warmth, thanking your hands for doing this healing work.

When you get in touch with disowned emotions, healing can begin. —FE

MANTRA: ***I release all emotion that no longer serves me. I step into alignment with the life I desire and deserve.***

EMPTINESS

"We mold clay into a pot, but it is the emptiness inside that makes the vessel useful."

—Lao Tzu, *Tao Te Ching*

How can we even remotely begin to fathom emptiness—a space free of judgment, sensory stimulation, and extrapolations of what is? Simply contemplating emptiness opens a space that can be filled with thoughts, ideas, and calculations of what the void contains. To free the mind from all projection and find the usefulness in emptiness's infinite potential, we must contemplate the value that can be found in vacancy by entering the void.

Let us try a breathing exercise, so that we can connect to this space as we reconcile duality with every inhale and exhale and find a sacred connection to present-moment awareness.

Step 1: Close your eyes and take note of any sensations you may currently be feeling in your body, heart, and mind. Acknowledge any thoughts that may be present inside, and say in your mind's eye, "I release, I relax, I let go."

Step 2: With every inhale, visualize a bright white light clearing away all thoughts, clearing away all judgment, and clearing away all obscurations of the mind as the light radiates and emanates through every cell of your body and every fiber of your being. With every exhale, let go of any heaviness, any doubt, any fear, releasing darkness and density, allowing them to absorb back into the cosmos, imagining that the darkness is transformed into beauty and its power is fueling space to hold billions and billions of stars.

Step 3: Continue this breathing pattern until you feel all sense of self, identity, and perception dissolve into dark matter—silent, dazzling darkness—and become enraptured in the appreciation of emptiness as the container, which holds the potential for all creation.

Step 4: Float in this emptiness and allow this energy to defragment all subconscious clutter as your thoughts organize on their own, without force or effort—only beautiful, empty space, organizing for you without any resistance.

Step 5: Open your eyes and take note of any feelings, sensations, or downloads you may have received while holding these visions of emptiness.

Did you find a resolution or revelation? Record any insight you may have received, and see how it may present itself on your path today. —JS

MANTRA: ***My mind is an open door to empty space. Where there were once thoughts, only the elegance of stillness remains.***

EQUANIMITY

"If we allow our thoughts to arise and dissolve by themselves, they will pass through our mind as a bird flies through the sky, without leaving a trace." —Dilgo Khyentse Rinpoche

Equanimity, as a superlative state of being, is present in many wisdom traditions, philosophies, and Eastern as well as Abrahamic religions. This word relates to maintaining inner stability and mental calmness, even through exposure to adversity and challenge.

In today's fast-paced world, it can be hard to maintain balance when everything moves with such dizzying speed. Yet, if we look to the past as a teacher of the present, perhaps we can find presence in the way we relate to time.

When Gautama Buddha sat under the Bodhi tree and awaited his enlightenment, he was faced with various degrees of temptation from the demon Māra, the Lord of the Senses. Through each challenge, Buddha maintained equanimity, never wavering from his center.

If you've pulled this card, the exercise below will help free your mind from temptation and connect your heart and spirit to the presence within equanimity.

Step 1: Close your eyes and begin taking note of your breath. Notice any tension or tightness that may be in the body; acknowledge any thoughts, judgments, or preconceived notions, and let them all go with every exhale.

Step 2: Inhale, visualizing an electric blue lotus opening in your inner eye, every petal pulsating with electricity, clearing away all obscurations of thought, spirit, and mind. This electricity is like a lightning bolt of consciousness, ridding all fear, doubt, and uncertainty.

Step 3: Exhale and release the current, grounding the electricity back into the Earth.

Step 4: Inhale, again visualizing this electric blue lotus pulsating and radiating with brilliant light, clearing away desire, heightened emotions, hunger, thirst, or physical want.

Step 5: Exhale and release the current, grounding the electricity back into the Earth.

Step 6: Inhale, again visualizing this electric blue lotus pulsating and radiating with brilliant light, clearing away attachment to outcome, attachment to opinion, attachment to bias, judgment, and negativity.

Step 7: Exhale and release the current, grounding the electricity back into the Earth.

Step 8: Inhale, again visualizing this electric blue lotus pulsating and radiating with brilliant light, emanating from the top of your head; down your neck and spine; throughout your arms, fingers, legs, and feet; beaming brightly through every cell of your body. Allow the lotus to explode into pure energy and dissolve into your inner space.

Step 9: Exhale and release the current, grounding the electricity back into the Earth.

Step 10: Open your eyes. —JS

MANTRA: ***My spirit emanates with the presence of radiant equanimity. I am enlightened in my own Buddha Nature, whatever the weather, temptation, or circumstances may be.***

FORGIVENESS

"Forgive others, not because they deserve forgiveness, but because you deserve peace."

—Jonathan Lockwood

Forgiveness equals freedom and peace of mind. It comes from a place of valuing your own energy first and recognizing your **own** power to heal **and** to hurt.

When you hold on to anger, resentment, sadness, and spite, it's as if you are holding on to heavy rocks. The person you feel this toward isn't also holding the rocks . . . only you are.

But you can let go!

Do your best to remember that people behave in a way that is reflective of their relationship with themselves and the experiences they have had.

Forgive as much as you can, because we are all truly doing the best we can according to our level of awareness. —KG

MANTRA: ***I love, I forgive, and I release all attachment to what was, so that I may fully embrace what is.***

FRICTION

"If you are irritated by every rub, how will your mirror be polished?" —Rumi

The Buddha often spoke of how our mental fetters, or attachments, are the source of the human plight of suffering, shackling us to the infinite phases of life, birth, death, and rebirth. This ongoing cycle, which is called Samsara in Hindu and Buddhist tradition, spins the human soul through rotations of lives and lessons, which are meant to aid us on our quest toward enlightenment. Each transmigration and transformation of life is a piece of a greater puzzle, fitting together what is yet to be resolved through revolution and greater resolution. Each reincarnation is a response to how we've imprinted time with our choices. The goal is to merge with Nirvana as we expel the mistakes of our past (and path) and exorcise our inner demons.

We are here on this Earth, experiencing our unique, precious lives, for purposes that can at times be a puzzle with an infinite number of pieces that seem challenging to "peace" together.

If we view each moment as a metaphor, the story of our lives becomes a history riddled with myths of our making, and each chapter carries consciousness closer to greater phases of creation. Love, anger, sadness, fear, doubt, beauty, and joy all take on new meaning. With a metaphorical mindset, we can view the gradients of our humanity as teachers meant to give light to the spaces of darkness within our spirit that need to be better understood.

Friction, as a teaching card, asks us to see where in life we can take what feels abrasive, and find the diamond within the coal. Simultaneously, within this teaching, we are asked to breathe deeply into what may feel out of focus, and have faith that a greater picture will emerge through time and directed intention.

In order for a match to be lit, it must strike against an opposing force strong enough to ignite a spark. Dominoes tumble only after the first is pushed. For a gemstone to emerge from a rock, it must first be tumbled. Magnificent statues materialize from marble only after what is not meant to be is chipped away.

Allow friction to polish your mirror today, and reflect more deeply on how contrast may actually be a great tool of liberation, while also remembering peace will inevitably emerge, just as all lessons piece themselves together in time. —JS

MANTRA: ***Friction can be a force for freedom, found through time and experience. I allow my inner and outer mirror to reflect authentic beauty amidst the unclear and mysterious.***

GRATITUDE

"We are never more than one grateful thought away from peace of heart."

—Brother David Steindl-Rast, *Gratefulness, the Heart of Prayer: An Approach to Life in Fullness*

If you've ever spent time traveling to different countries or immersing yourself in unfamiliar cultures, chances are you discovered new perspectives beyond the framework of what is most familiar to you. An appreciation for ancient cultures or brave new worlds can lead to eye-opening discoveries that capture a new perspective and bring what's important into focus. The new experiences that can be found through adventuring beyond what we consider home are here to remind us that there's more to life than just the material and the familiar. Cultivating gratitude for the kaleidoscope of human experiences can allow a smile of presence to overflow from your heart and ripple forward into your overall appreciation for life. When you look beyond and meet new, unfamiliar faces and ways of being, you'll discover something we are all universally fluent in—a smile.

It can often feel as though today's world has been designed to detract us from simplicity, as the rapid pace of modernity only further feeds the complexity of the human experience and continues to entangle us with distractions. It is easy to forget the power that exists in appreciating something as simple as the warmth that comes from a smile, even if that smile is from a stranger. Negativity can creep in when we get too lost in our distractions. It can infect the mind with toxic thoughts and cynicism. However, there is a simple and effective way to combat the negative thoughts that haunt us, and that is with a gratitude practice.

When you feel those negative thoughts begin to weigh you down, pause. Just pause. Take a moment and think instead of things you are grateful for. This is how you train the mind to shift toward gratitude when it is tempted to think negatively.

There are so many things to be grateful for. Can you sit with gratitude for the gifts you have? That may be a safe place to sleep at night, friends to call, a phone to call them with, books to read, internet access with infinite information to be learned, having any of the five senses, or even the opportunity to overcome the challenges you are facing.

If you think you don't have time to take five minutes to do this practice, just remember that the parenting, the job, the chores, and whatever else you need to get done will be done even better with this new perspective.

Start by expressing gratitude every morning. That's it. You can begin with something as simple as, "Thank you so much for letting me wake up this morning happy and healthy."

Take note of how your life changes and how your perspective continues to shift by living from this heart-centered space. —FE

MANTRA: ***I awake each morning with a grateful heart. I am happy, I am healthy, and I am ignited with life's sacred spark.***

GREATNESS

"Never underestimate the power of dreams and the influence of the human spirit. We are all the same in this notion. The potential for greatness lives within each of us."

—Wilma Rudolph

To be great we must recognize that we already are.

We must look ourselves in the eye and understand that our true greatness, our unfathomable power, lies within our potential, dormant and waiting to awaken. Greatness is not something that's achieved; it's something that you accept and actualize.

This card is here to remind you that you **are** divine greatness!

With this awareness, you can move away from feelings of insecurity, jealousy, and inner conflict. Instead, you will now move forward from a space of understanding, love, and self-acceptance.

Walk with your greatness. It is not in the past, nor in the future, but with you now. —KG

MANTRA: ***I accept, embrace, and activate the power of my greatness.***

HARMONY

"In harmony, everything succeeds."

—African proverb

When we are in true harmony, we achieve inner peace and can see with clear awareness.

If you pull this card, it's important for you to take time to listen to the echoes of the universe and pay attention to what you're experiencing in your body.

Ask yourself, are you in harmony with your heart, body, and mind?

Are you trusting your intuition?

Are you negatively judging the encounters you're having by interpreting them through your own negative biases?

Pause and observe the movement around and within you.

Make a commitment to be more in harmony with the source of all things, the universe, your soul, and your physical body. You might be surprised by what you discover and find resonance with! —KG

MANTRA: ***I live in harmony with my spirit, heart, and mind. I resonate with childlike awe when I think of the universe's sacred design.***

INITIATION

"If you want to know your past life, look into your present condition; if you want to know your future life, look at your present actions."

—Sogyal Rinpoche, *The Tibetan Book of Living and Dying*

Initiation is a process of spiritual growth, where we enter into a rite of passage, a ritual, or an experience that changes our consciousness and redirects the trajectory of our life's path. Through each advancing degree of wisdom, a new understanding of the world and the cosmos emerges, allowing a greater sense of perspective to evolve. Mystery schools, both ancient and modern, employ this method for candidates seeking to join a group of seekers on the path to transcending consensus reality, while other traditions practice this idea to commemorate a passage into adulthood and the official joining of a community.

Initiation can be considered a portal of ascension between who you once were and who you are meant to, or deeply desire to, become. It is a rebirth into the world, with new awareness, knowledge, and embodied wisdom. It is an alchemical process of dissolving illusory ideas in order to see with new eyes and move past any previous mirages of mind with embodied spiritual maturity.

Certain mystery schools will not only encourage but also require silence on the path to advancement, so as to not allow the opinions of others to tamper with the process of your inner workings. Outside voices can distract, in stereo, and cause the process to be muffled with the ideas and judgments of the uninitiated.

If you've connected to the Initiation card, you may currently be going through a process of metaphorical "death," ending what **was**, to begin what **is** or could **be**. You're advancing on your life path, inching closer to your soul's calling, and the experiences you're currently walking through are heightening your senses, sensibilities, intuition, and imagination. It may feel like things are speeding up and time is transforming to timelessness. If so, connecting to your breath and finding a relationship with stoicism may assist in advancing through any challenging growing pains and identifying projections before claiming them as ultimate "truth."

Once you walk through this mysterious door of perception, what you may find on the other side is an expanded vision of the world, galaxy, universe, and creation as a whole. Your heart, spirit, and mind are the metaphysical skeleton keys that will continue to unlock new doors of your innerverse as space expands with you. —JS

MANTRA: ***I accept the cost it takes to walk the path. I value every moment and experience as I reflect within my spirit's looking glass. I choose to advance with courage through this test in life's great class, and know the impact I make with my action is built to last.***

INTENTION

"This mind is the matrix of all matter."

—Max Planck

There are two ways to look at intention: through ego or through spirit. Ego says, "I will force this thing to happen with my power." Spirit confidently states its intention, then surrenders to something greater and trusts the process. Your higher self also trusts that if the intention does not manifest, it's because what does show up in your life is for your highest good.

Science has taught us about atoms—the building blocks of life. But can it be true that atoms (or that which we focus on) can change through our intention?

According to the notable German scientist Max Planck, there may be a conscious intelligence shaping those atoms.

While accepting the Nobel Prize in 1918, he said, "All matter originates and exists only by virtue of a force which brings the particle of an atom to vibration and holds this minute solar system of the atom together. We must assume behind this force of existence is a conscious and intelligent mind."

A 2020 study published in the journal *Nature Communications* and carried out by psychologists at Queen's University in Kingston, Canada, estimated that the average person has 6,200 individual thoughts per day. So when you say affirmations like, "I am free from all financial limitations," there are hundreds of thoughts countering that by saying, "No, you're not." That is why it can be helpful to set an intention, something like, "I set the intention for financial freedom, so that I may use the abundance I create to help cultivate a better world." It has a different vibration that the mind will more likely accept. Your brain goes, "I set the intention to be financially free, and I want to help other people (not just myself). Okay, I can get behind that!"

Financial stability is nice, of course, but you can also start with small daily intentions. For example, every morning, try stating, "I intend to have a wonderful and fulfilling day."

Let's take a look at another example. A crystal necklace is beautiful and charged with healing energy; if you were given one as a gift, it would be very precious. But there are many ways it could have been offered to you. It could have been handed to you or thrown at you. It's the same gift, but given with a different intention. If it is handed to you, it is a gift, but if it is thrown at you, it becomes an insult. The same goes with your daily work and actions. Offer your work in service of creation, and its meaning changes. —FE

MANTRA: ***Intention is the vehicle that fuels my desire into being. I trust that my confidence in believing will call forth the reality that I would like to see.***

INVOLUTION

"The mind acts like an enemy for those who do not control it." —*Bhagavad Gita*

We all have a monkey mind, which the Buddhists consider to be the "unsettled; restless; capricious; whimsical; fanciful; inconstant; confused; indecisive; uncontrollable" parts of our consciousness. This aspect of the human mind makes us feel as though life happens **to** us and not **through** us. Our thoughts can often feel like they are not our own, and yet we must remember that we can still choose at every moment which thoughts are being fed by our energy. Evolution is the concept of life undergoing gradual development and growing into something new, and can be used as a potent metaphor for our inner and outer journeys. Involution, as an esoteric concept, can be viewed as the process of integrating the growth of our consciousness in conjunction with the growth of our living universe.

Your mind is a playground of expression; awareness travels through this playground and believes anything you tell it. This is the moment to construct your thinking!

What we are thinking about most, and how we think about these things, will create what we experience and how it affects others. If you hone in on what you attend to, you can experience single-point focus and the ability to direct your awareness. This gives you the mental fortitude to complete any task you desire, so if there is something you have left unfinished, now is the time to cultivate this talent and push it through to the finish line.

Step 1: Find a point on a wall and lock your eyes and the energy center right above your eyebrows on it.

Step 2: Commit to being fully present in this moment; let this be the most important task you could possibly be doing. Fully, and wholly, release into the now.

Step 3: Begin to breathe in through your nose for 5 seconds and out through your nose for 5 seconds, finding a rhythmic breath as you focus your full attention on the point on the wall that you chose.

Step 4: As you breathe in, imagine that you can breathe across the room and completely take in the area you are staring at.

Step 5: Exhale and send this breath and energy out of you and back to this point, continuing to breathe 5 seconds in and 5 seconds out.

Step 6: Do this for a total of 22 breaths, the exhale and inhale being one breath.

You have completed the purification of your mind and have taken back your ability to direct your focus and choose what you wish to bring energy to.

Take this heightened awareness and apply this breathing pattern to anything that you do and you will have the energy, concentration, and flow to be able to achieve whatever you decide. —BW

MANTRA: ***I breathe in focus and release stagnation. I commit to using my awareness to play an active role in my life's creation.***

KINDNESS

"Kindness will never be wasted in any way."

—Japanese proverb

"Give the love you wish to receive" is a very powerful yet simple statement. We often unconsciously train ourselves to make what we lack into something we subconsciously worship, and forget the power of love as something we can pay forward and experience through a cycle of reciprocity.

Rather than wasting time thinking about what we don't have and fixating on all that we are lacking, what if we used that time to shift our energy away from our own inner struggles? What if we focused our attention on how we might be more loving and generous to others who may be in need?

This card is a reminder that when you are inspired to give love, do not hold back. Now is the time to be the miracle, so that when you need one in the future, you know they are possible because you yourself have been exactly that for someone else. Your actions have the potential to spark a cycle of reciprocity and encourage new ecosystems of positive energy exchange.

A single candle can light an infinite number of flames, and by acting in kindness toward others, you're practicing, by direct experience, the power of your own divinity. When you emanate from this space of divinity, you ignite a divine spark, which will guide you to learn new things about yourself and continue to expand your field of awareness by being in loving service as you move through the world, and make an impact on those around you.

Nothing is placed in your experience by accident; each time you interact with someone, you are choosing a story line within an infinite universe of possibility. So what character are you going to play in their book of life?

Are you a dakini (an embodiment of enlightened energy), or a hungry ghost (a being tormented by insatiable desire)?

Are you an angel, or a demon?

Are you an extra, or are you just a non-player character?

Are you the star, or a production assistant?

Are you the reader, or the writer?

What are you creating within the field of creation?

You are being asked to bring more kindness into the world, enjoy the process of creating miracles, and be a miraculous presence. Shift from fear to love by sparking kindness with embodied action and authenticity. —BW

MANTRA: ***With simple acts of kindness, I kindle the fire of a thousand flames. With this light of inspired action, I emanate pure love. Where there was once darkness, only light remains.***

KINTSUGI

"Everything has beauty, but not everyone sees it." —Confucius

Kintsugi is a Japanese art form (and philosophical outlook) in which what is "broken" is repaired with precious metals, such as gold, platinum, and silver. As a living philosophy, breakage and subsequent repair are viewed as beautiful even in their brokenness. An object's history is its own poetry in static motion, and perceived "flaws" only add to the unique preciousness of the vessel, which has undergone change through time and direct experience.

When we perceive something as damaged or broken, the initial shock of something beloved no longer being what it **was** can cause a visceral reverberation through the heart space. Feelings of attachment tethered to affection and nostalgic waves of longing can cause deep suffering, and our shattered emotions may cause us to burst into tears in sympathy with what is believed to be broken. This can leave us feeling as though we've been shattered into a million pieces, left wondering how we can get ourselves together to face tomorrow, let alone face today.

Yet, if we seek compassion and view what feels like brokenness through the lens of creative catharsis, we allow space for something new to emerge. Brokenness is healed by precious connective tissue, gold found in the lessons, and the new pattern that materializes. Object and subject are no longer separate, but equally healed with awareness and imagination.

In moments where you may feel broken, empty, and in need of repair, remember that the brokenness can contain a layer of unexpected beauty, especially when we consciously attempt to weld the spaces of emptiness with preciousness.

In alchemical metaphor, Mind (often referred to as "The All") has the ability to turn lead into gold through transmutation. In the metaphor of embodied art, kintsugi is here to remind us to find the lightness of being and to transmute the tough moments in life into tremendous works of art with the consciousness of the master craftsman.

If you pulled this card and are feeling broken today, in any way, remember the art that you are, and that there's always a space for a new masterpiece (or master of peace) to emerge. —JS

MANTRA: *I weld the pieces of my past back together with gold, and stand in my presence as a work of art to behold. What was no longer is, and what will be is beautiful.*

KNOW THYSELF

"You are not a drop in the ocean; you are the entire ocean in a drop." —Rumi

They say to know thyself is to know God.

Not the self as in your human identity, but the self that is unseen. The invisible self that you walk with, that observes your experiences.

Be mindful of that presence.

Take the time to get to know your true being, and trust that the answers are within you. This true you is not influenced by the constructs of human conditioning and is always ready to be present. Knowing this true you better will bring you closer to infinite consciousness by reminding you that you are a part of a much bigger energy that is having a conversation with itself. —KG

MANTRA: ***I am a precious drop of life's infinite ocean, and this indivisible infinity sets the abundance of my life in motion.***

LIBERATION

"By liberation of the self through love, we will develop love." —Gautama Buddha

Before we can achieve liberation, we must look at what is currently keeping us from our ultimate freedom.

What layers of expectation are we confined to?

If you had complete liberation right now, would that even be something that you would be willing to accept?

We often seek comfort and familiarity in order to avoid the discomfort of change.

This card is a gentle nudge to take a step into the unknown, away from what feels comfortable, and pivot from your usual choices so you can get closer to freedom. Remember that you, in fact, are already liberated, but it is the human conditioning that we use as our blueprint that hides how truly free we already are. —JS

MANTRA: *It is my right to be liberated from that which limits my mind. I believe in my inherent freedom and leave all limitations behind.*

MAKTOUB

"It is not life that's complicated, it's the struggle to guide and control life."

—F. Scott Fitzgerald, *This Side of Paradise*

"Go with the flow" is a piece of advice that may feel difficult to wrap our brains around, especially when things feel particularly challenging. How can we flow with the current of life when we may constantly feel as though we are treading water, attempting to avoid the riptide, and doing whatever we can to stay afloat? How can we establish a greater sense of trust when the ripple of reality feels overwhelming?

Well, what this concept essentially means is to consciously let go of any resistance that may be occurring when it comes to trying to control the circumstances in our lives, and to, instead, use the tools we have to navigate nebulousness with faith.

Maktoub in Arabic translates to "it is written," and it is the idea of predestination or destiny. In other words, God/Creator/Source (whichever name you feel most comfortable with) already knows everything that ever was and ever will be, because it has already been written in the sacred book of this life experience.

What comes our way may not always be in our hands, but how we respond can be. It often appears that life is an accident, but perhaps it is actually a culmination of past karma, unconscious creation, and the butterfly effect of our greater connectivity.

Going with the flow does not mean that you just sit back idly, because, again, you have the power to be in control of your response to any situation! If stones are thrown at you, don't shirk away or hide in a sense of smallness. Build a castle with those stones instead of a prison.

While the unexpected that comes your way is not always within your conscious decision, what you make out of it can be.

This card is here to remind you that you have the power to chisel and shape your reality. Never forget that you already have all the tools you need to do so.

So, how will you respond to what life brings your way? What is your decision? What will you build? —FE

MANTRA: *I flow with fate, but also understand my conscious freedom to mold, shape, and create each day of my life. I choose to be an architect of experience, to embrace the wisdom of the mysterious and the sacredness of creation's light.*

MASK

"Man is least himself when he talks in his own person. Give him a mask, and he will tell the truth." —Oscar Wilde, *The Critic as Artist*

At this moment, you are being asked to consciously play with the many forms, or avatars, that you have the potential to embody. The Mask card has presented itself as a reminder that now is the time to design and refine your character so that you can take flight and spread your creative wings. This freedom will allow you to openly express the many experiences you have collected up until this point, by consciously molding a character that is an amalgamation of your own active imagination. It is time to configure your character into an archetype that feels unique and special to you so that you can method-act your new expression on the world's great stage of possibility.

Sometimes we must attempt something we have never done before to reach the next stepping-stone on our path. First, try connecting to what feels like the most authentic version of yourself and watch with curiosity as the world responds to this new iteration of **you**.

Negativity may creep in at this stage, but you can reroute thoughts simply by saying, "I can do anything" or "I am that I am."

Dream the biggest dreams you could possibly dream at this phase, as the stepping-stones bring us closer to our highest excitement. Dig deep into what feels new and exhilarating, and allow yourself to transform into this brilliant shimmering of potential as you dazzle the world with your highest expression of self.

Perhaps this may even look like creating an experience, or going somewhere you always wished you could go! Release all judgments of the unknown and see if you can perceive things for the first time, while also playing with the many expressions that are you.

We are not our body or our thoughts, and when we release the idea of who we think the world wants us to be, we can finally be FREE! Explore what that freedom looks like today and which "mask" you wore (or took off) to get there. —BW

MANTRA: *I can do, and become, anything I choose. I now choose to embody the avatar of my highest excitement, and the mask I now wear brings me closer to a feeling of enlightenment and my truest "me."*

MODERN

"Any sufficiently advanced technology is indistinguishable from magic."

—Arthur C. Clarke, *Profiles of the Future: An Inquiry into the Limits of the Possible*

There can be two different types of people in this world: those who contemplate the philosophies of the past, and those who dream of the future that is yet to be born.

Which one are you?

Come close and let us tell you a secret: You can be, and hold, both time lines, and all is able to be accessed at any time!

The old is rooted in ageless wisdom, understanding that the plants, animals, cycles of nature, and universe can be our greatest teachers. Meanwhile, the new is rooted in innovation, fast-paced technology, computer code, and the ability to harness the power of modern resources to magnify the mind's intention.

Some Indigenous healers may look upon modern technology and see destruction of the old, while others may see it as creation, with the ability to shape new cycles of creativity, and nature's own intelligence working its way through human nature's intelligent minds.

However, if all circumstances in life and death are karmically perfect, then the modern world must fall under that umbrella of divine perfection. There are no accidents; there is no such thing as sheer coincidence.

Destruction comes when we use the modern resources we've been given to cause harm rather than for the betterment of all sentient beings. Your phone carries the ability to play angry music, yet it can also play high-vibration frequencies. Your laptop can stream violence, or it can stream inspirational and soul-nourishing documentaries. Cinema can inspire dreams of greater tomorrows or cause us to have nightmares and restless sleep.

Technology can be a black hole or a portal, a weapon or a tool, a source of creation or destruction, and **you** get to decide which one it is.

How will **you** use all the resources available to you today?

Will **you** create or will you destroy?

Will **you** weaponize or build?

What metaverse will **you** create within this ever-unfolding universe of potential?

The Modern card is here to remind you to choose wisely and use the resources available to you with discretion, mindfulness, and loving awareness. Synthesize the wisdom of the ancients with the machinations of the modern, and there you'll find a bold new sense of balance. —FE

MANTRA: *I can merge ancient wisdom with the modern world. I can be a sage of technology while also being attuned to the lessons in nature and the intelligence of Mother Earth.*

NIRVANA

"Your mind is Nirvana." —Bodhidharma

If you hold a lit candle in your hand and look at its shadow on the wall, you'll notice the shadow of the candle, but not from the light of the wick's fire. Blow out the candle, and the shadow remains, but the invisible fire will have turned to smoke, rising and evaporating back into the atmosphere.

The human spirit is an ephemeral shimmering of light, flickering for a finite amount of time on Earth before advancing to the great, mysterious beyond.

Nirvana, in Buddhism, literally means "blowing out" or "quenching." When we contemplate this idea in relation to the ultimate attainment on the other side of our cycles of experience, how do we release attachments to the life span of our light without being burned by what we cling to?

As an exercise, let's release some of the "fires" that are sources of attachment and suffering on the path to liberation.

Step 1: Close your eyes, and take an extended inhale through your nose. As you inhale, visualize any moments in life where you may have been greedy, possessive, or deeply attached to a particular object or sensory experience. Visualize this feeling as a fire in your mind's eye.

Step 2: Strongly exhale through your mouth like you're blowing out a candle. Visualize the fire being put out with your breath as you extinguish that energy, and allow all residue to evaporate away from your life-force.

Step 3: Take another elongated inhale through your nose. As you inhale, visualize any moments where you may have been ignorant, judgmental, or extremely attached to an idea. Visualize these moments as a fire in your mind's eye.

Step 4: Strongly exhale through your mouth like you're blowing out a candle. Visualize the fire being put out with your breath as you extinguish those moments, and allow the residue to evaporate away from your life-force.

Step 5: Take one more deep inhale through your nose. As you inhale, visualize any moments in life where you may have held anger, hostility, or resentment toward another person, place, or experience. Visualize these emotions as a fire in your mind's eye.

Step 6: Strongly exhale through your mouth like you're blowing out a candle. Visualize the fire being put out with your breath as you extinguish those emotions, and allow the residue to evaporate away from your life-force.

Step 7: Open your eyes and take note of your feelings. —JS

MANTRA: *I am light, but my fire does not burn. I maintain grace as the wheels of karma turn. Nirvana is my goal every day on this path, and I understand that my impact, not this vessel, is what's here to last.*

NOURISHMENT

"Remember to take care of yourself. You can't pour from an empty cup." —Unknown

These three simple words can go a very long way: "How are you?"

Right now, you are being asked to reflect on how you're truly feeling, and what you're currently doing to take care of yourself.

The Nourishment card is here to remind you to practice self-care any way you can! Eat good food, dance, draw, sing, jump, move, treat yourself! Now is the time to nurture your mind, body, and soul, and this card is asking you to do something today to fill your cup back up.

There is an ancient Chinese practice that advises leaving 30 percent in the tank (for example, leaving a party when you are having the most fun) so that you don't completely tap your energy resources and are still left wanting more.

Everyone needs something different in order to feel healthy and whole, so find what works for you and devote yourself to it today, even if it's just lying on your back breathing on the ground, reconnecting with your heart.

Your intuition knows what you need, so be open to following it. Life is not just about what you do, but how happy you are when you get to participate in each life experience. Therefore, in order to magnetize your dream experiences, you must remember to focus on how your core energy is being sustained and how much happiness you can imbue into your highest intentions.

Pulling this card may also serve as a warning that you might be unconsciously on autopilot and missing out on life. This happens to us all throughout the course of our lives because our brain loves to conserve energy through repetition. Unfortunately, we aren't naturally programmed to always do what's best for us, but instead what's convenient and comfortable.

Practice life as a moment-to-moment mastery of presence and awareness. This is much easier done when you have the life-force energy to do so, so take today and make it unapologetically yours.

Enjoy breathing in life as you experience the best it has to offer. Nourish your heart fully, and wholly. —BW

MANTRA: *I fill my cup with joy and love, so that when others need me, I can be fully present and aware. I am worthy of nourishment as a form of self-care.*

ONE

"You learn by reading but understand by LOVE." —Shams Tabrizi

Ubuntu is an Nguni Bantu term that recognizes the interconnectedness of humanity. "I am, because we are," or "humanity toward others" begs us to remember that the nature of our humanness is inextricably linked.

Oftentimes when we search for answers, we forget how much we already know. Simply by looking within, we can be reminded of the interconnectivity that we all have with one another. Once we connect to this consciousness and drop into absolute harmony, the answers will rise.

The connection that we have with nature, humanity, and everything within consciousness is one.

Remember your power and deep connection to everything and every **one**, and allow that awareness to shine. —KG

MANTRA: ***We are one, and I am, because we are. As I connect with my inner light, I remind others to remember who they are.***

PARTNERSHIP

"Love conquers all; let us too surrender to love." —Virgil

To be in partnership is to be in union, but it requires clear communication and patience.

Partnerships can exist in a multitude of ways.

Are you being the best partner to yourself right now?

Are you being the best partner to your loved ones?

To your family?

To your business acquaintances?

This card is asking you to meditate on what kind of responsibility you are taking in regards to how you are showing up as a partner.

You are being led to reflect on partnership because there might be something that you are seeking an answer for that requires more commitment.

Be committed to being a better partner to yourself and to those around you, and watch your relationships blossom. —KG

MANTRA: ***I commit to honesty, humility, and being the best partner I can be.***

PERCEPTION

"O mind, abandon this perception of diversity and realize the unreality of your own independence from the infinite consciousness: this is liberation."

—Swami Venkatesananda, *Vasistha's Yoga*

Imagine yourself walking with a friend in a beautiful, luscious park and coming across a captivating tree.

You might think, "What a marvelous tree filled with a vast array of colors." Meanwhile your friend finds it unremarkable and comments on its scrawny branches and lackluster shades. The truth is that the tree is neither marvelous nor lackluster, it just is. In that state of being, it is perfect in itself, yet we project our own perspectives onto what we think it is.

We tend to do this every day with everything, every encounter, and almost every moment, as our judgment casts a mirage onto the images we process with our vision and inner landscape. When you pull the Perception card, it is important to notice how you may be doing this with the current situation you're facing, and how you can alter the way you are looking at what's in front of you. Whatever difficult transition, challenge, or moment in time you are experiencing right now, you can say, "I am willing to see this differently." You can, without using force, open your mind to see what shifts in perception may occur and how you can recalibrate your focus through this simple alignment of vision and intention.

Perception is not reality, but rather our projection onto reality.

Consider the circumstance you're dealing with today and recognize that you, and you alone, give it all the **meaning** it has. It, whatever it may be, is the outward projection of your inner thoughts, and its meaning is what you are making it. When we recognize that our thoughts, words, and visions inspire and affect our outer world, we can take responsibility for the way we work with our senses and refine our sense-making abilities. We can become more conscious creators, liberated from projection, and empowered in the shifting of creation. —FE

MANTRA: *I see what I wish to see, and these visions empower me to create my own reality. I understand that projection is an illusion, and I free myself from poisonous thoughts. I use my mind's eye to create magical potions of awareness that remind me of my inner power and clear away all toxic mirage.*

THE PHILOSOPHER'S STONE

"I am the wisest man alive, for I know one thing, and that is that I know nothing."

—Socratic Paradox

This card is here to help you appreciate the wisdom that exists in knowing nothing, and yet, much like the Fool card of the Major Arcana, you have access to all information.

Soften into this present moment, and from this space you will find the silence to unlock your intuitive gifts. Here is the path to get you there:

The philosopher's stone is a concept, and material, that is used to alchemize various forms of matter and mind into higher vibrational tools. Today you are recognizing yourself as this tool and instrument for spiritual sustenance.

Step 1: Soften your soul and relax wherever you are sitting.

Step 2: Begin to feel the texture of your breath as you deepen and lengthen it.

Notice that there is energy that comes into your body while you do this.

Step 3: Exhale fully and slowly breathe in the energy of the ground. Feel your body become heavy.

Step 4: Deeply listen to your surroundings, and let each sound and sensation take you within yourself.

Step 5: Rest in the silence.

Step 6: Open your body up fully, and practice paying attention to different vibrations in your environment: the wind, sky, earth, ambient sounds, silverware clanking . . . whatever is around you, listen to it.

Step 7: Breathe these frequencies into your body and feel them loosening up and transmuting any tension felt.

Step 8: Soften and let go fully.

Step 9: Repeat breathing in different vibrations that you hear to alchemize your emotions, and then allow your imagination to run freely. You can imagine anything and use that frequency to heal, elevate, and transcend your current state.

This is a powerful practice that has the potential to unite you with all things. Even the most negative vibration, when opened fully, can be used as a huge release. You also have the capacity to send energy and healing to others with your breath.

Ask permission first, and if their soul says yes, be fierce in how you give your love. Now is the time to step into your power as the magi and healer that you are, and creatively attune how you use your gifts. Remember to keep it light, because you are light. Have no resistance to what is, and remember that the more you give, the more you receive. —BW

MANTRA: ***I transmute negativity into radiance, and alchemize my reality with the warmth of the sun, transforming darkness and density into golden, loving light.***

PRISM

"You are what you believe in. You become that which you believe you can become."

—Bhagavad Gita

When light moves through a prism, it is refracted by the angles and shape of the object. Because of the nature of its geometry and structure, it is able to take solid white light and separate it into a spectrum of differing colors. A rainbow emerges from a singularity at the speed of light, only after passing through mirrored three-dimensional reality.

The Prism card asks us to reflect on this metaphor, on the current shape of how you're relating to a single thought or idea. Have you found yourself stuck in a myopic point of view, unable to release shackles of uncertainty, defeat, or limiting belief?

The prism is here to remind you that whatever is feeling like a single-minded perception can be bent into boundlessness by seeing into the spectrum of potential that exists within whatever time line we choose to participate in. The various rays of reality can color our experiences with new realizations and ideas that radiate iridescence.

Pain has the potential to be transmuted through the prism of humor if we look at the shades of adversity from a different angle. Levity is there waiting for us to discover the magic of comedy and the crazy wisdom in absurdity, if we are able to bend our beliefs and adapt our mindsets.

If you can find the courage in your heart to fully face what you fear, perhaps what you'll find beyond the apparition is merely a hungry ghost in need of love and compassion. Treat your demons to cookies and tea; you may see that they're just angels in disguise, and a caring heart can cauterize prior wounding and projections of density.

Belief has a prismatic effect on thought, and if you move through what is containing, or constraining, your ability to find momentum, you may find an infinite variety of possibilities within the refracted rainbow of reality. —JS

MANTRA: *I paint my reality with a bold spectrum of colorful shades. I allow experience to be filtered through a prism, which shows me the wisdom within every color grade. I can bend light, with love as a force of my will. The rainbow of life is here to show me that my life's journey doesn't always need to be a battle uphill.*

PROTECTION

"The best lightning rod for your protection is your own spine." —Ralph Waldo Emerson, *Lectures and Biographical Sketches*

Whenever you're feeling vulnerable to negativity, it is important to seek protection. You can do so through meditation—praying to your angels, guides, and ancestors.

Protection also requires you to look internally and connect with your intuition. Begin trusting, observing, and listening to the voice inside.

Call in whatever spiritual forces that align with your beliefs and remain diligent in your efforts toward peaceful resolve.

Sometimes the difficulties you face can be great teachers, yet other times you may be facing an energetic blockage. It's important to recognize the difference so you understand when to have grace through conflict, and when to pick up your metaphysical sword and armor. —KG

MANTRA: ***I am protected by forces of love and light, and in this protection, I am able to discern what is actually mine, and what isn't my fight.***

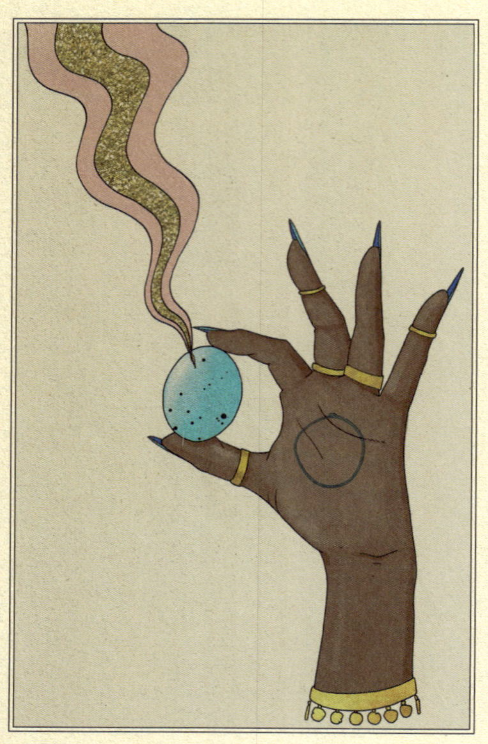

REBIRTH

"When your light shines purely, you will not be born, and you will not die."

—Gautama Buddha

Rebirth is one of the most powerful cards you can pull because it offers the entirety of fortune's wheel of possibilities—anything can happen, anything could happen, everything is happening.

The universe is currently creating the space for your biggest dreams to manifest in reality, and everything that has led you to this moment happened for you to experience what's next.

Directing your awareness toward what you want and taking action from inspired love will assist you at this time of great rebirth. To completely be reborn is a long and courageous path, and this card is assuring you that it's all coming together. —BW

MANTRA: ***I breathe in passion and release trepidation. I am prepared for rebirth and accept my auspices as part of this new movement into inspired action.***

RECIPROCITY

"The best way to find yourself is to lose yourself in the service of others."

—Mahatma Gandhi

When you switch from a paradigm of self-serving to that of helping others, success, value, and purpose will almost always follow in direct response to the goodwill you offer to the world. When you enter into this ideal, you inspire the energy of reciprocity, which is a cycle of positive action and an exchange of kindness begetting even more kindness.

Even something that may seem mundane, like inputting numbers into a spreadsheet day in and day out, when offered with an intention to serve, shifts into something meaningful and fulfilling.

Even something as simple as helping someone with their groceries, opening a door, or offering assistance in what may feel like a "small" way can have a big impact on someone's life.

Martin Luther King Jr. said, **"Not everyone can be famous, but everyone can be great, because greatness is determined by service."**

In a world where many will admire others for nothing more than being famous, the truth is, ten years from now, most of us won't be able to name the cast of our favorite reality show but will still remember Mother Teresa and Mahatma Gandhi, because of their life's impact in service to humanity.

Selflessness withstands the test of time.

Every life you touch creates a potential for more kindness to emerge.

Reciprocity comes in response to the new cycles you'll inspire through acts of loving-kindness.

Like the seed of hope that springs from a flower only to sprout roots and allow life to blossom again in time, when you offer a flickering of hope when things may feel hopeless, you help to breathe more beauty, and love, into the world, which is desperately needed.

Every bit of impact you make in your life matters. There's no use in comparing yourself to others when it comes to your own acts of kindness and how you choose to give back to the world. There are great souls all over the planet who are changing lives, helping others, planting trees, and regenerating the environment, and we will never get to know their names. Their greatness is measured by the weight of their actions, and their ripple of impact, not by the size of their social media following.

Take the situation you are dealing with today, or whatever issue may be before you, and dedicate it to the intention of reciprocity, then watch what happens in the days ahead. Pay it forward, and what comes back to you will be a spiritual treasure that is absolutely priceless. —FE

MANTRA: *I care for the well-being of others. I practice acts of selflessness and kindness in assistance to my universal sisters and brothers.*

REFLECTION

"For those who have an intense urge for Spirit and wisdom, it sits near them, waiting."

—Patanjali, *The Yoga Sutras of Patanjali*

Everything you see—everything—is a reflection of your inner world, thoughts, and intentions. What if the ancient sages were right, and you could change your outer world simply by changing your inner world through self-reflection and clear intention?

What are your beliefs about money? Does it come easily and effortlessly, or is it never enough and always lacking?

What do you feel about the world? Is it a safe and peaceful place filled with loving people? Or is it a scary, dangerous place filled with greedy people who are only interested in themselves?

How do you feel about others in general? Are you open to meeting new friends and exploring the potential for beautiful new relationships? Or are you cynical, critical, pessimistic, and constantly placing judgment on the minutiae?

How do **you** feel, period?

And how are these beliefs being reflected back at you?

These questions, and many more like them, can be avoided for a long time, but they eventually will need to be confronted. This process of confrontation can be uncomfortable at first, but the more you dive deeper into self-reflection, the more you witness and correct your inner vision, the more you'll begin to see how certain patterns and beliefs have dictated your life. Just like going to the gym can be difficult at first, but you slowly become stronger and more accustomed to the routine, self-reflection gets easier and more routine once practiced regularly. It's a muscle that you can stretch and grow with the proper time, attention, and nourishment.

If meditation isn't your thing, you can also ask your subconscious mind some questions and take a little bit of time to close your eyes and contemplate the answers you receive. When you're ready, write your revelations down in a journal. It's important that you don't react by writing down the first thing that comes to mind, but rather respond to the question by taking your time to truly contemplate what you're receiving.

Here are some questions you can ask yourself:

Who am I, really?

What do I want?

What am I avoiding? What am I afraid of?

What am I grateful for in this life?

What are my gifts that I would like to share with the world? —FE

MANTRA: *I reflect on clarity and am open to receive the answers I need. I am ready to accept the advice and embody the wisdom I receive.*

RESISTANCE

"Live with cause and leave results to the great law of the universe. Pass each day in peaceful contemplation." —Zen koan

Chinese finger-puzzles are a gag toy that "imprisons" an unsuspecting victim's index fingers inside a small cylindrical object made of lightly woven bamboo. Once trapped, the typical reaction is to attempt to break free from the puzzle by abruptly pulling away, and to avoid capture by resisting the confines of the object. With every pull in the direction of opposition, the grip of the trap only gets tighter. The paradox of the puzzle is that escape can only be found in surrender and release.

The action of pushing toward the middle of the cylinder and moving away from resistance is where liberation from this prison may be ultimately found.

This finger-puzzle is a dynamic metaphor for how the act of resistance and opposition can leave us feeling trapped, in a panic, or stuck struggling out of a situation that we've initially, and perhaps unconsciously, consented to. We may find usefulness in considering the act of surrender when met with feelings of resistance, and lean into the notion of less being more. Gentleness is a force all its own. We can break free from what we are attached to only with the proper, and intentional, movement.

The more we pull away from the confines of the objects that bind us, the tighter they will grip onto our ability to expand and evolve. The more we struggle for freedom, the more freedom will become a struggle.

Where is resistance coming up in your life? What does liberation feel like to you? How can you let go of what is binding or blocking your energy, and flow into a sense of freedom?

You have the power to resolve resistance with solvent thoughts. Move closer to equanimity by breaking free from your fears through gentle confrontation. May the lessons that emerge in moving closer to inner (and outer) liberation allow you to shed limitations and shift focus to expansive vision. —JS

MANTRA: *As I move closer to areas of resistance, I find that in this space, I will actualize my freedom. Where I once felt trapped, I am now in full liberation from all fear, doubt, and indecision. I am a force of gentleness, and I move and flow with divine precision.*

RESOLUTION

"You think you have won! What is light without dark? What are you without me? I am a part of you all. You can never defeat me. We are brothers eternal!" —*Legend* (1985)

When contemplating the myths, stories, and tales of fantastical worlds throughout the human zeitgeist, we can see a common theme of "resolution" being found in the slaying of the dragon, the killing of the villain, or the death of the antagonist as the means to the end and the way to the happily ever after.

Perhaps it would be boring if the realms of the fantastic didn't end with a battle scene or "Final Boss," but how much of this programming has found its way into our subconscious minds? How does it affect our outlook on resolution of extreme conflict from the metaphorical and personal journey of life?

The "Darkness" of our times can often feel like a Titan, a tentacular monster with arms that crush the human spirit, a bogeyman that haunts our greatest fears, an all-consuming Nothing, a shadow looming and clouding hope for the future.

How can one even consider something so complex and titanic as the foreshadowing of future time lines yet unseen? How could we get to the top of our metaphorical Mount Doom to defeat Sauron?

In J.R.R. Tolkien's book series *The Lord of the Rings*, the protagonist hobbits show us that no matter how big or small you are, you can still be the hero of your story. Even the smallest form of life has the potential to change everything . . . every thing has the potential to change.

Similarly, Atreyu, a young boy, saved Fantasia in Michael Ende's *The Neverending Story*. Just as for him, there's no easy answer to the epoch we are traversing, because victory comes not from defeat, but from resolution, regeneration, and a greater revelation in how inextricably linked every form of life is.

Light and dark are two sides of the same coin.

Cycles may be destined to repeat.

There and back again.

Instead of slaying our dragons, what if we, perhaps, learn to tame them, ride them, and guide them? What if we find the humanity in Dr. Frankenstein's monster without chasing it with a torch?

Resolution not in defeat, but in resolve.

Allow the power of your imagination to be the element that has the potential to mold, shape, and guide what's yet to come.

Here and into the future. —JS

MANTRA: *I invoke the power of my imagination as a tool for ultimate manifestation. I resolve contrast, and contradiction, with the understanding that duality is but an illusion of the interconnected nature of all conditions. I appreciate my shadow, and embrace my light. I know that love is a greater emotion than fear and fright.*

THE ROSE PHOENIX

"Be bold, and mighty forces will come to your aid." —Basil King, *The Conquest of Fear*

Today you are stepping into spiritual completion. You have done the work to heal the past and are becoming more and more masterful with managing your emotions in the present.

The future you that has all the answers and has already accomplished its mission for humanity is able to send you energy across time and space for you to be nourished and empowered now.

Like a rosebud, you have fully blossomed, and like a Phoenix you are rising from the past, flying fearlessly into an inspiring horizon.

Step 1: Create a rose in your mind—even if the image comes quickly, spend some time filling in the details and creating each petal. Put each neutral, positive, and negative thought into the rose. Watch this rose expand in your mind's eye, and then explode it to create space.

Step 2: Breathe in and out 10 times through your mouth as if you are breathing through a straw, inhaling the mystery of life and exhaling all stuck emotions from the body.

Step 3: Set an intention for whatever information you need right now to best assist your journey to cultivate the greatest good for not only your soul, but the planet at large.

Step 4: Ground yourself into your body and envision the highest incarnation of yourself sitting in front of you.

Step 5: Watch their breathing pattern. How do they breathe life? Where are they breathing from? Begin to mimic the depth and frequency of their breath.

Step 6: As they exhale, feel the color and energy of their field come out of their mouth. Breathe their energy into your body and exhale it back to them. Watch them breathe you in. After a couple of moments of this, watch their body and yours merge into one. Soften into the energy and just be.

Since you have completed the healing process, you've now called upon your highest time line to be the truth of your experience. Know that it is, and trust the intuitive knowing that will naturally express itself through you. —BW

MANTRA: *I've merged with my highest time line, and completed an important phase of my healing path. I trust that all the work I've done on my spirit and mind is solidified and built to last. Beautiful as a rose, but protected by time's thorns, where I once was lost, I am now fully reborn.*

SQUARING THE CIRCLE

"Celestial messengers, we shall wander in immensity, and the stars will be our gleaming ships."

—Éliphas Lévi, *The Key to the Great Mysteries*

In alchemy, the metaphor of "squaring the circle" relates to mastery over our inner and outer operations.

Understanding the correspondences in nature and in mathematics, the master alchemist can see the relationship between that which is above and that which is below, that which is within and that which is without.

They are able to see the significance of all the changing seasons, the wisdom in the differences of the elements, and the intelligence in the directions. Becoming one with the four, their vision is whole, as all transitions of time are fully appreciated.

As a conceptual meditative practice, let us incorporate this idea into a breathing technique called Box Breathing, as we seek to master our minds and operate from the grace of self-mastery.

Step 1: Inhale through your nose while slowly counting to 4. Feeling the air fill your lungs and visualizing the current of energy moving upward, repeat in your mind's eye, "As above."

Step 2: Hold your breath for 4 seconds.

Step 3: Slowly exhale through your mouth while slowly counting to 4. Letting all the air out and visualizing the current of energy moving to the right, repeat in your mind's eye, "So below."

Step 4: Inhale through your nose while slowly counting to 4. Feeling the air fill your lungs and visualizing the current of energy moving downward, repeat in your mind's eye, "As within."

Step 5: Hold your breath for 4 seconds.

Step 6: Slowly exhale through your mouth while slowly counting to 4. Letting all the air out and visualizing the current of energy moving to the left, repeat in your mind's eye, "So without."

Step 7: Repeat as many times as you'd like until you feel a sense of completion. —JS

MANTRA: *I am one with the elements, seasons, directions, and sky. I am complete in my understanding of the infinite and perfect* why. *I've squared the circle and see life with the philosopher's mind. There's gold in this perspective, and I appreciate this clarity of my inner eye.*

STRENGTH

"An ant on the move does more than a dozing ox." —Lao Tzu, *Tao Te Ching*

Strength is not just measured by how much we can literally hoist or hold. It can also be a metaphysical quality, measured in emotional, mental, and spiritual fortitude, especially during times of fear, doubt, and uncertainty.

To remain strong when you feel powerless against unexpected and relentless waves of change requires a certain level of trust in your abilities to surf the currents of time with graceful balance, rooted in your center.

Achieving an adept level of core strength doesn't always come easily, but the more we work on it, the more it will work for us and grant us the ability to achieve equilibrium and stable footing.

No matter how big or small we may *feel*, a potent metaphor to remember is that even though an ant is tiny, it is able to carry up to fifty times its own weight. Beyond the physicality of strength, if we consider our part in the grand scheme of the cosmos, we are but a speck of sand in this vast cosmic sea, yet our actions have an impact even on a microcosmic scale.

With this perspective, we are reminded that we carry a great weight each day of our lives, because of how we are able to fold both time and space through the movement on our beautiful yet laborious journey through the human condition. We can move mountains and build monuments with our mind through intention, planning, and the strength to follow through.

Our condition is not measured in literal heaviness, but in the symbolic voyage that either makes us, breaks us, or takes us to bold new horizons as the micro factors into the macro, and the macro feeds into the meta.

This card is a reminder that strength can always be accessed, even when you're feeling weak. By looking deep within, you'll come to find that you'll never be without. The mind is a powerful tool that can help you transcend all obstacles if you trust the assistance it can offer.

When you need the greater reminder, simple yet potent affirmations like "I am strong,"

"I am powerful," "I am capable," or purely just "I am" will help recalibrate thought patterns away from weakness and into power.

Focus on your fortitude, and you will soon discover fulfillment. —JS

MANTRA: *If I look within, I will never be without. I am strong enough to transcend all of my fears and doubts.*

SYNTHESIS

"Imagine a multidimensional spider's web in the early morning covered with dew drops. And every dew drop contains the reflection of all the other dew drops. . . . And so ad infinitum. That is the Buddhist conception of the universe in an image." —Alan Watts

The metaphor of Indra's Net stems from both Buddhist and Hindu cosmology, and relates to the metaphysical concept of non-duality. Indra is a Vedic deity who is believed to be the God of the heavens and of the Devas (gods). His net is infinite in dimension, and within this web is a structure of infinite multifaceted jewels, and within each jewel, all other jewels are reflected.

Imagine a precious lattice of life, where all action is reflected, connected, and inter-dependent upon the actors. A worldwide web of multidimensional movement, which echoes through infinity.

The Hegelian dialectic is a philosophical thought exercise where a point (thesis) is met with a counterpoint (antithesis) and inevitably a compromise (synthesis) arrives.

As a meditation, let's visualize Indra's net as the connective tissue between action and response. Every jewel holds the reactions and reverberations, and the perception of it all is the compromise, because we, as perceivers, are still limited in our projection as we traverse through the illusory nature of reality.

Step 1: Close your eyes and visualize a crystal spider, however it may come to your mind's eye.

Step 2: Once you see the spider, imagine it weaving a web that begins with an action you've recently done and perhaps felt poorly about. As the web starts to form a pattern, contemplate how the response to that action resonated in your reality.

Step 3: Next, in your mind's eye, imagine a gentle rain beginning to fall. See drops of water landing on the web. Look at each "jewel" and see what's inside. Ask it to show you the reverberation and reaction of your actions through the landscape of time.

Step 4: Contemplate what you see.

Step 5: Zoom out until you can attain an eagle-eye view of this vision in your mind's eye. Witness the spider, the web, the drops of water within the pattern, and take note of how you feel when you observe this scene.

Step 6: Open your eyes and record any thoughts or feelings. —JS

MANTRA: *I strive for perception, and acknowledge my part in the greater cosmic connection. I see, but understand there's always more than what meets the eye. Infinity is ever-present, even when it may be in disguise.*

TEACHERS

"I have learned silence from the talkative, toleration from the intolerant, and kindness from the unkind; yet, strange, I am ungrateful to those teachers."

—Kahlil Gibran, *Sand and Foam*

Not all teachers have classrooms, and some of life's greatest lessons can come from friends, unexpected moments in time, synchronicities, people you may not agree with (or like), and even perfect strangers on the street.

Some of those lessons may emerge from the most uncomfortable situations. In fact, some of the absolute best lessons can come from those moments in time!

Even those folks who just rub us the wrong way or trigger unresolved wounds are revealing something deep, or hidden, about ourselves, especially when we shift focus and witness the teaching at hand.

The greatest teachers don't preach to you, don't talk at or over you, but instead lead you to the lesson through a journey of self-discovery, as you reflect on the great cosmic mirror of interconnectivity.

They show you where to look, as Kahlil Gibran said, "but do not tell you what to see." When someone does something to upset you, they are showing you where to look, but it's up to you what lesson you'll choose to see.

For instance, if someone never responds to your emails, and you find yourself getting angry with them, maybe the lesson is that you need to give yourself a break, take a pause, and disconnect.

Perhaps you're constantly pointing out little mistakes a friend is making, and maybe the lesson is that you are too critical of others and need to give them a break.

If someone isn't as available with their time and attention as you'd like, maybe, instead of taking it personally, the greater lesson is that you also need to cultivate better boundaries and protect your energy in ways that allow time to work well for you.

Pause, pay attention, and take note of what this moment is teaching you right now.

Where is the lesson, where is the reflection, and how can you integrate this learning into your continued evolution as you become the best version of yourself?

This card tells you to honor your teachers today, and complete your metaphorical homework by studying and applying all that you've learned along the way. —FE

MANTRA: *I see a lesson in every reflection, and honor all of the teachers in my life. Good, bad, or indifferent, I appreciate the curriculum of my daily classroom and all of the cosmic insight.*

TRANSCENDENCE

"Wherever you go, go with all your heart."

—Confucius

This card is here to let you know that you are entering a shift in your awareness and are elevating beyond your usual point of view into a space of transcendence.

You will begin to see the forest through the trees.

Things that always looked one way might start to look a little different now.

The paradox will flirt with you, and you'll respond in kind.

What was once big is now small, and what is small will seem enormous. You'll see a speeding up of signs in the physical and dream realm—please pay attention!

Transcending isn't always comfortable and can sometimes feel alarming, painful, and overwhelming. Rest assured that you're supported through the shift. —KG

MANTRA: *I embody the energy of transcendence in heart, spirit, and mind. I trust all signs and embrace the new energies I continue to find.*

WEIGHTLESSNESS

"Undisturbed calmness of mind is attained by cultivating friendliness toward the happy, compassion for the unhappy, delight in the virtuous, and indifference toward the wicked."
—Patanjali, *The Yoga Sutras of Patanjali*

Are you often finding that you are weighed down by your own ideals of how things need to manifest, staying fixated on your wants and attached to the outcome you've embossed inside your mind?

When we find ourselves in a place of consciousness like this, we create static noise where there should be harmony. Our expectations for our desires, for others, for ourselves, and how we feel life ought to be creates a heaviness that lends itself to more difficulties as we question the why and how of things, instead of appreciating what is and allowing divine timing to show up as it intends.

This card is here to remind you to be weightless, to let go of expectation by finding beauty in acceptance and remaining unburdened by opinion, projection, or the notions we cling to.

The reason to remain positive and not burdened with negativity is not so that everyone can see you from a superficial perspective of seeming radiantly happy all the time. Instead, it is an important inward journey to be weightless so that you can move more quickly to your goals with the help of your invisible support system.

A feather is easier to move than a rock.

Fanning small flames can help them burn brighter, while a gust of wind can extinguish the light.

The perfect breeze can direct a sailboat into its best charted territory, while a storm can take it far off course.

Water's softness can erode the hardest surfaces in time.

Being weightless means that whatever comes at you, you have full faith and trust that it is in your best interest. You know this is all for your benefit, so you accept it and you allow the blessings of the experience to blossom without force.

Being weightless means not being burdened by your own and others' expectations of outcomes. It means you float freely and with effortless ease, trust, and acceptance. Allow yourself to become so weightless that you may become truly untethered from attachment and stay open to the coincidences and serendipitous moments in your life. —KG

MANTRA: *Weightless, I float through life with effortless ease. Like a dandelion, I move gently with the breeze. My heart is feather-light, and my spirit is full of stars. I effervesce with loving awareness, appreciating everything as its own work of art.*

ACKNOWLEDGMENTS

To my husband, Adam. Your love is my greatest treasure, your heart is so precious, your smile is everything to me.

Natalee, thank you for being the best creative partner, friend, and artistic muse I could ever ask for!

Anna, without your support, and grounding, I wouldn't be where I am today. Thank you for helping this project (and many more to come) become a reality.

Frank, thank you for being an anchor point and a bright star in the constellation of this beautiful collaborative vision with Kat and Bryant.

To Rythmia, thank you for opening the portal that allowed this work to begin, and complete.

—Jennifer Sodini